Understanding Disabilities

Understanding Physical Disabilities

JESSICA RUSICK

Big Buddy Books
An Imprint of Abdo Publishing
abdobooks.com

abdobooks.com

Published by Abdo Publishing, a division of ABDO, PO Box 398166, Minneapolis, Minnesota 55439. Copyright © 2022 by Abdo Consulting Group, Inc. International copyrights reserved in all countries. No part of this book may be reproduced in any form without written permission from the publisher. Big Buddy Books™ is a trademark and logo of Abdo Publishing.

Printed in the United States of America, North Mankato, Minnesota.
052021
092021

THIS BOOK CONTAINS RECYCLED MATERIALS

Design: Emily O'Malley, Mighty Media, Inc.
Production: Mighty Media, Inc.
Editor: Megan Borgert-Spaniol
Content Consultant: Brenda Blackmore, Special Education Director
Cover Photographs: shorrocks/iStockphoto (child in wheelchair), Shutterstock Images
Interior Photographs: duaneellison/iStockphoto, p. 17 (top left); FatCamera/iStockphoto, pp. 5, 7, 13 (top); Francesca Diaco/Wikimedia Commons, p. 14 (top); JohnnyGreig/iStockphoto, p. 13 (bottom); kali9/iStockphoto, p. 21; Shutterstock Images, pp. 4, 6, 8, 9, 10, 11, 12, 16, 17 (top right, bottom), 18, 19, 20, 22, 23, 24, 25, 27, 28, 29; SolStock/iStockphoto, pp. 15 (top), 17 (center); Sport the Library/Wikimedia Commons, p. 15 (bottom); sweetmonster/iStockphoto, p. 14 (bottom)

Library of Congress Control Number: 2020949917

Publisher's Cataloging-in-Publication Data
Names: Rusick, Jessica, author.
Title: Understanding physical disabilities / by Jessica Rusick
Description: Minneapolis, Minnesota : Abdo Publishing, 2022 | Series: Understanding disabilities | Includes online resources and index.
Identifiers: ISBN 9781532195761 (lib. bdg.) | ISBN 9781098216498 (ebook)
Subjects: LCSH: People with disabilities--Juvenile literature. | Physically challenged people--Juvenile literature. | Disabilities--Juvenile literature. | Social acceptance--Juvenile literature.
Classification: DDC 362.43--dc23

CONTENTS

Just Like Others 4
What Is a Physical Disability? 6
Motor Skills 10
Types of Physical Disabilities 12
Mobility Aids 16
Physical Disabilities at School 18
Social Struggles 20
Being a Friend 22
Strengths 26
Golden Rules 28
Activities 29
Glossary 30
Online Resources 31
Index 32

Just Like Others

It's Mia's first day of school. Mia has a physical disability that weakens her **muscles**. So, she uses a wheelchair. In the hallway, kids stare at Mia as she passes. They seem unsure of how to talk to her.

Sometimes, other kids **assume** Mia is sad about her disability. But Mia is proud to be who she is. She loves hanging out with friends and going to the park. She also loves playing basketball. Mia wishes more kids understood that she is just like them.

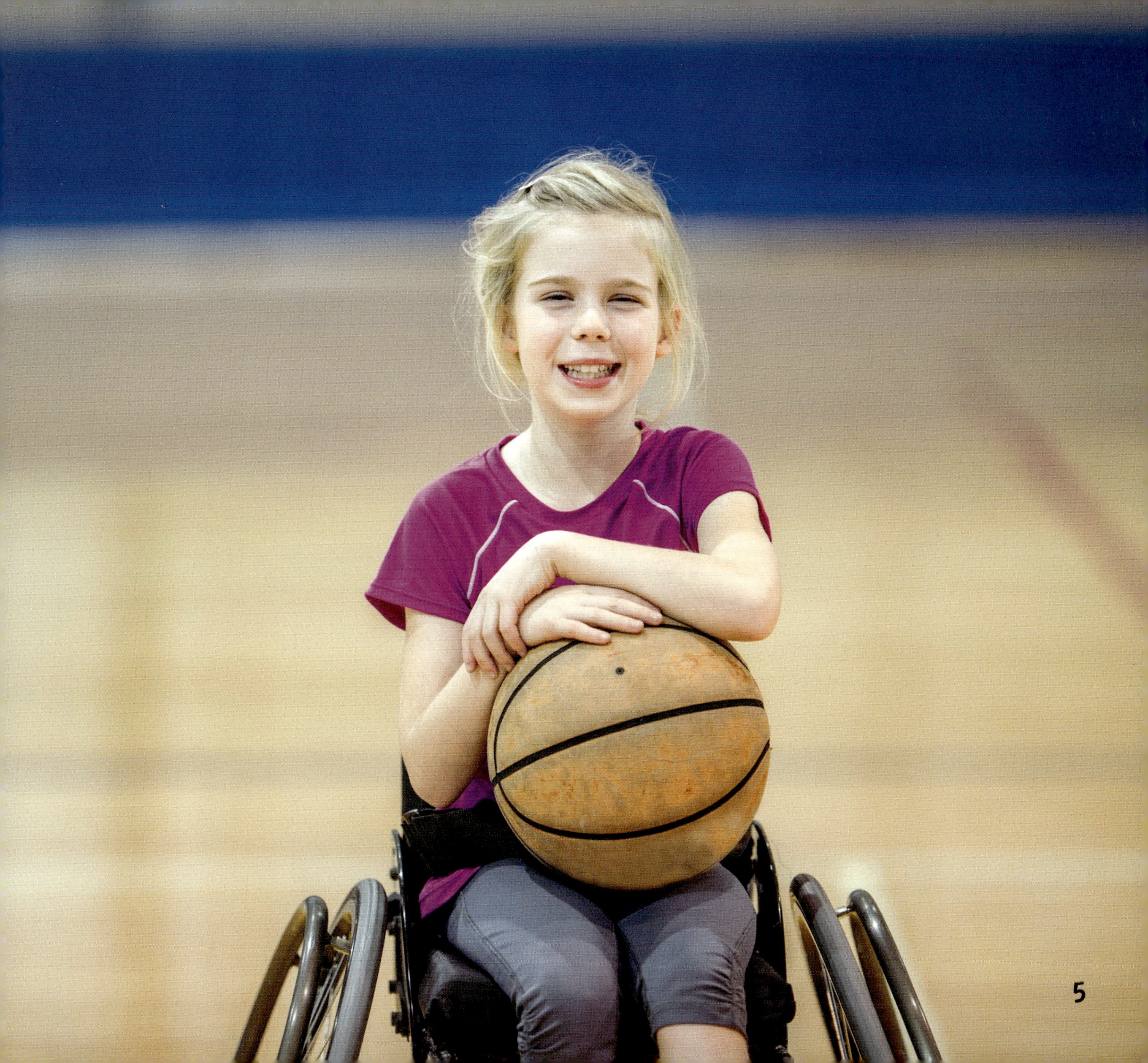

What Is a Physical Disability?

A physical disability affects how a person moves and controls his or her **muscles**. People with physical disabilities may have trouble standing, walking, or sitting up without help. They may also have trouble **gripping**, holding, or lifting things.

It's important to accept and **appreciate** people's differences. You can show you accept and appreciate others by trying to learn more. You might politely ask if they'll share how their physical disability affects them.

Some kids with physical disabilities work closely with special helpers during the school day.

Always use respectful language. Name-calling is never okay. Also be sure to avoid incorrect terms. For example, someone who uses a wheelchair is not "**confined** to a wheelchair" or "wheelchair-bound." This makes it sound like being in a wheelchair is limiting. Wheelchairs give users **mobility** and freedom. So, simply say that someone "uses a wheelchair."

Remember

People with disabilities are not **victims**. This word makes it sound like having a disability is a bad thing. But a disability is not bad. It's just a difference!

Be sure to respect how a person with a physical disability chooses to **identify**. It's best to ask which kind of language a person prefers.

I am a person with a physical disability.

Person First

Person-first language puts a person before his or her disability. People who use it believe people should not be defined by their disabilities.

I am a physically disabled person.

Identity First

People who use **identity**-first language believe someone's disability is an important part of his or her identity. Some physically disabled people prefer to identify as such.

Motor Skills

Often, a physical disability affects a person's motor skills. A motor skill is a movement that requires using the **muscles**. There are two types of motor skills. They are gross motor skills and fine motor skills.

Gross motor skills use large **muscle** groups, like those in the arms and legs. These skills include:

- ★ Raising arms
- ★ Standing
- ★ Walking
- ★ Running
- ★ Climbing
- ★ Kicking
- ★ Jumping

Fine motor skills use small muscles, like those in the hands. These skills include:

- ★ **Gripping** objects
- ★ Waving
- ★ Getting dressed
- ★ Tying shoelaces
- ★ Writing
- ★ Using scissors

Types of Physical Disabilities

Some people are born with physical disabilities. For others, physical disabilities are the result of an **accident**, **injury**, or illness.

Different physical disabilities affect different parts of the body. Some common physical disabilities include:

Cerebral Palsy (CP)

CP is the most common physical disability in children. It affects the ability to move and control **muscles**. People with CP may have stiff or uncontrolled movements. They may also have poor balance.

Muscular Dystrophy

Muscular dystrophy causes a person's muscles to become weaker over time. People with this disability often have trouble moving with control. They may also trip and fall often.

Osteogenesis Imperfecta (OI)

OI makes it hard for the body to form strong bones. People with OI may break bones easily. They may also have bones that are not formed normally. This can make movement **challenging**.

Spina Bifida

Spina bifida causes a gap in a person's spine. Some people with this condition have weakness in their legs. Others cannot move their legs. This is called **paralysis**.

Amputation

Amputation is the removal of a **limb**. It can happen because of **injury** or illness. Some people are born without a limb or part of a limb. This is called **congenital** amputation.

Spinal Cord Injury

A **spinal cord** injury affects the ability to control **muscle** movements. Some spinal cord injuries cause **paralysis** below the neck. Others cause paralysis below the waist.

Mobility Aids

Some disabled people use **mobility** aids to help them move and balance. There are many different types of mobility aids.

Wheelchair

Some wheelchairs are moved forward by the user or another person. Other wheelchairs are powered by electricity. These can be controlled by a user's hand, chin, or mouth.

Forearm Crutches

Forearm crutches have cuffs that wrap around someone's arms or wrists. The crutches help **support** a person while walking.

Leg Braces

Leg braces are metal **supports** that wrap around the legs, ankles, and feet. They help support weakened **muscles** when a person walks.

Walker

A walker is a three-sided frame on wheels. Users **grip** the walker for balance as they walk.

Stander

A stander supports someone in a standing position. Many standers have trays. Users can rest their arms or place objects on the trays.

Artificial Limb

An **artificial limb** replaces a body part that is missing. It can be made of plastic, metal, and more.

Physical Disabilities at School

Many **devices** help disabled kids do well in school. For example, some disabled kids may find it hard to use pencils. So, they may use devices that change spoken words into written words.

Some kids with physical disabilities have classroom aides. These are people trained to help kids complete work and do activities during the school day. Some kids may also leave class for in-school **physical therapy**. This can help some disabled kids improve their **mobility**.

Classroom aides work with individual students or small groups.

19

Social Struggles

Kids with disabilities are more likely to be bullied. That's because other kids see them as different. Being bullied makes people feel bad about themselves.

Kids with physical disabilities may also feel left out of group activities. That's because other kids may not know how to include disabled peers. Or, they may **assume** that kids with physical disabilities can't join in. Being left out makes people feel lonely.

Kids with physical disabilities can play all kinds of sports. And many sports can be adapted for disabled players.

Being a Friend

Everyone has his or her own strengths and **challenges**. That's okay! No matter what, everyone should be treated with respect.

There are many ways to be a good friend to someone who is disabled. Ask your friend if she wants to share what it's like having a disability. If she does, listen respectfully.

And, think of ways to include your friend in activities. Sometimes, she may need to take part in a different way. If you're unsure how your friend can join in, ask an adult for ideas.

Find common interests with kids you know who have physical disabilities.

23

More Ways to Be a Friend

Ask First

Ask before helping your friend. Sometimes, he may welcome help. Other times, he may not need it.

Stand Up to Bullying

Tell an adult if your friend is being teased.

Respect Personal Space

Don't touch your friend's **mobility** aid without asking. A mobility aid is part of someone's personal space.

Strengths

Having a physical disability can be **challenging**. However, some people believe their physical disabilities make them more **determined** and accepting of others. There are actors, doctors, sports stars, and more with physical disabilities.

Ali Stroker

Ali Stroker is an actress and singer. At age two, Stroker's **spinal cord** was harmed in a car **accident**. As a result, Stroker uses a wheelchair. She is the first wheelchair user to perform on Broadway. In 2019, Stroker also became the first wheelchair user to win a **Tony Award**!

Ali Stroker and actor David Perlow at the 2019 Tony Awards in New York City

Golden Rules

Millions of people have disabilities. If you know someone with a disability, there may be times when you feel unsure of what to say or do. When in doubt, remember to treat others how you'd want to be treated. And, keep in mind these other golden rules:

- Accept and respect differences
- Use respectful language
- Be kind and caring

Activities

Do you have a friend with a physical disability? Invite him or her to join you for a fun activity.

Watch a movie

Bake cookies with an adult's help

Go on a scavenger hunt around your neighborhood

GLOSSARY

accident—an unplanned event that may result in harm or injury.

appreciate—to value or admire greatly.

artificial (ahrt-uh-FIHSH-uhl)—made by humans.

assume—to think something is probably true without knowing enough about it.

challenging (CHA-luhn-djing)—testing one's strengths or abilities. Something that is challenging is a challenge.

confined—held or kept within a limited space.

congenital—existing since birth.

determined—having a strong feeling about doing something without doubt or uncertainty.

device—an object or machine that has a certain job.

grip—to hold tightly.

identify—to say or show who someone is.

identity—the set of features and beliefs that make a person who she or he is.

injury (IHN-juh-ree)—hurt or loss received.

limb (LIHM)—an arm or leg.

mobility—the ability to move or be moved.

muscle (MUH-suhl)—body tissue, or layers of cells, that helps move the body.

paralysis (puh-RA-luh-suhs)—a loss of the power to move or feel part of the body.

physical therapy—the treatment of disease or injury using massage, heat, exercise, or other physical methods.

spinal cord—a cord of nerves inside the spine that carries messages between your brain and your body.

support—to hold up or give help to someone or something. A support is something that holds up or gives help to someone or something.

Tony Award—an award that recognizes excellence in live American theater.

victim—someone who has been harmed by an unpleasant event.

ONLINE RESOURCES

Booklinks
NONFICTION NETWORK
FREE! ONLINE NONFICTION RESOURCES

To learn more about physical disabilities, please visit **abdobooklinks.com** or scan this QR code. These links are routinely monitored and updated to provide the most current information available.

INDEX

acceptance, 6, 26, 28
activities, 18, 20, 21, 22, 23, 29

being a friend, 22, 23, 24, 25, 28, 29
being respectful, 8, 9, 22, 25, 28
bones, 14

causes, 12, 13, 14, 15, 26
classroom aides, 7, 18, 19

devices, 18

identity, 9

mobility aids, 4, 8, 16, 17, 25, 26
motor skills, 6, 10, 11
muscles, 4, 6, 10, 11, 13, 15, 17

paralysis, 14, 15
physical therapy, 18

school, 4, 7, 18, 19
sports, 21, 26
strengths, 22, 26
Stroker, Ali, 26, 27

teasing and bullying, 8, 20, 25
types of physical disabilities, 13, 14, 15, 26